Festivals of the World

NIGERIA

Gareth Stevens Publishing
MILWAUKEE

Written by
ELIZABETH BERG

Edited by
KAREN KWEK

Designed by
HASNAH MOHD ESA

Picture research by
SUSAN JANE MANUEL

First published in North America in 1998 by
Gareth Stevens Publishing
1555 North Rivercenter Drive, Suite 201
Milwaukee, Wisconsin 53212 USA

For a free color catalog describing Gareth
Stevens' list of high-quality books and multimedia
programs, call
1-800-542-2595 (USA)
or 1-800-461-9120 (Canada).
Gareth Stevens Publishing's Fax: (414) 225-0377.
See our catalog, too, on the World Wide Web:
http://gsinc.com

© **TIMES EDITIONS PTE LTD 1998**
Originated and designed by
Times Books International
an imprint of Times Editions Pte Ltd
Times Centre, 1 New Industrial Road
Singapore 536196
Printed in Singapore

Library of Congress Cataloging-in-Publication Data:
Berg, Elizabeth.
Nigeria / by Elizabeth Berg.
p. cm.—(Festivals of the world)
Includes bibliographical references and index.
Summary: Describes how the culture of Nigeria is
reflected in its many festivals, including the
Argungu Fishing Festival and the Feast of Ogun.
ISBN 0-8368-2017-7 (lib. bdg.)
1. Festivals—Nigeria—Juvenile literature. 2.
Nigeria—Social life and customs—Juvenile
literature. [1. Festivals—Nigeria. 2. Nigeria—
Social life and customs.] I. Title. II. Series.
GT4889.N6B47   1998
394.269669—dc21   98-16238

1 2 3 4 5 6 7 8 9 02 01 00 99 98

CONTENTS

It's Festival Time . . .

Nigerian festivals are a burst of color and fun! From harvest celebrations to honoring their ancestors, Nigerians love to get together and enjoy themselves. A Nigerian celebration isn't complete without lots of drumming, dancing, and singing. Whatever kind of festival you like, you're sure to see the most amazing masked dancers. So get ready to party—it's festival time in Nigeria!

WHERE'S NIGERIA?

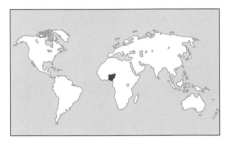

Nigeria has the most people of any country in Africa. It faces the Atlantic Ocean, where West Africa and Central Africa meet. The country is named after the Niger River, one of the longest rivers in the world. The capital, Abuja, is a new and modern city. People in Abuja live much like people in big cities anywhere. In the rest of the country, however, many Nigerians live the same way their ancestors did.

Who are the Nigerians?

About 250 different groups of people live in Nigeria. The Yoruba, Hausa, Fulani, Igbo, and Ijo are among the biggest groups. The Hausa and the Fulani live together in the northern part of the country. The Yoruba live in the rain forests and savannas of the southwest. The Igbo live in the rain forests of the southeast. Many Igbo and Yoruba are Christians, although a few still follow traditional beliefs. The Ijo live in the south. Long ago, these peoples all lived separately. They followed their own customs and rules. It has been hard for them to learn to live together.

A Nigerian girl with a doll tucked in her dress. In Nigeria, this is how mothers carry their babies.

4

NIGERIA

Zuma Rock in Abuja, Nigeria.

Map labels

CHAD

NIGER

N

Sokoto
Argungu
Katsina
Kano
Maiduguri

Sokoto

Niger

BENIN

Kainji
Reservoir

Kainji Lake
National Park

Zaria
Kaduna
Jos
Jos
Plateau
Kumo
Mubi

CHAD

Kaduna

Niger

Yankari
Game
Reserve

Benue

Yola

ABUJA

Ilorin

Benue

Oyo
Ogbomosho
Ibadan
Oshogbo
Makurdi
Katsina

Abeokuta
Ondo

Lagos
Benin City
Enugu

Niger
Onitsha
Cross

CAMEROON

Aba
Uyo

Port
Harcourt
Calabar

Niger
Delta

Gulf of Guinea

WHEN'S THE CELEBRATION?

Many Nigerian festivals do not follow a strict calendar. For example, Ijo **masquerades** take place whenever there's a need to honor that god or ask an ancestor for help. Other festivals take place any time before or after the harvest. Nigerians also celebrate important times in the life of a person. For example, initiation marks the passage from childhood to adulthood. Nigerian Muslims follow the Muslim calendar, which moves back 11 days every year. Their festivals change season gradually with the calendar.

Tired of studying? Come with us to page 12!

SPRING

✪ **ARGUNGU FISHING FESTIVAL**
✪ **GELEDE**—Celebrated to honor the great Earth mother and the women elders of the Yoruba.
✪ **EASTER**—Celebrated Nigerian style, with **elaborate** religious processions.
✪ **EGUNGUN**
✪ **FESTIVAL OF THE NEW YAM**
✪ **FEAST OF OGUN**—During this festival, a procession of respectful drummers and servants surrounds the Oba, or King.

SUMMER
⊙ OSHUN FESTIVAL

AUTUMN
⊙ NATIONAL DAY—Celebrates the anniversary of Nigeria's independence from Great Britain on October 1st.

Hey! Bring a friend! You're invited to a party on page 16!

WINTER
⊙ CHRISTMAS—An important festival for Nigerian Christians, Christmas is celebrated with processions, church services, and masquerades.

⊙ UTUAK NDOK (END OF THE YEAR CELEBRATION)—The Ibibio live mostly on the western side of the Cross River. Their New Year takes the form of a wind sweeping through the land, carrying evil spirits, ghosts, and misfortunes to the sea.

MUSLIM FESTIVALS
⊙ ID AL-FITR

⊙ ID AL-KABIR—Celebrates the return from the Hajj, the pilgrimage to Mecca that is required of all Muslims. Muslims sacrifice a sheep to show their willingness to sacrifice everything for God.

⊙ ID AL-MOULOUD—Celebrates the birth of the Prophet Muhammad.

HONORING THE GODS

The Yoruba have 420 gods, so you can imagine how many festivals they have to honor them! Each of these gods is different, and their festivals vary, too. However, most of them include three very important things—no traditional Nigerian celebration is complete without masks, dancing, and drumming!

Masked Egungun dancers celebrate in the streets.

Egungun

The biggest festival of the year for most Yoruba is *Egungun* [ee-GOON-goon]. It honors the spirits of the ancestors and asks for their help. The festival lasts for several days. Each **clan** celebrates on a different day. On the clan's day, dancers representing the ancestors of the clan dance through the village. The dancers wear a special costume made of many layers of cloth strips. The costume covers the entire body. When the dancers jump and twirl, the strips flip over, showing the other side. The dancers must bring the costume to life with their dancing. Then, they no longer seem like ordinary persons—they have become something from the Other World!

This Yoruba woman invites you to join in the dancing!

Shango

One of the favorite Yoruba gods is *Shango* [SHAN-goo]. Shango was one of the early kings of the Yoruba, so he is like an ancestor who became a god. After he died, people began to think of him as the god of thunder and lightning. Because Nigeria has many **destructive** storms, it is important to honor Shango. At his festival, a male dancer goes into a deep trance, and the god takes over his movements. The dancer's arm movements are lightning-quick, and he rolls his shoulders to show the power of thunder.

This Yoruba chief is inspecting a row of wooden figures dedicated to Shango, the great god of thunder.

9

Honoring the mothers

The Yoruba believe women possess great power. They celebrate Oshun, the river goddess of fertility, in the town of Oshogbo. The high point of the festival is when everyone jumps into the river to bathe and collect holy water.

Other Yoruba women also enjoy special treatment. Old women—along with goddesses and female ancestors—are called "our mothers." They control the fertility of the land and the people. It is very important to keep the mothers happy, so that crops and children will grow.

Opposite and *above:* Shrines dedicated to Oshun, the Yoruba goddess of fertility.

Left: Yoruba women are feared and respected for their power over life and death.

Think about this
Many peoples of different cultures from all over the world believe in an Earth goddess who controls the fertility of the land. She is often quite a powerful figure, and the people fear and worship her. Can you think of other ways that people honor the Earth mother, or make her happy in times of trouble?

SHARKS AND WATER SPIRITS

L ife on the Niger Delta continues today much as it did hundreds of years ago. In this land of marshes, rivers, and mangrove swamps, villagers busy themselves with farming or fishing. Life is peaceful and quiet—most of the time.

Suddenly a loud cry goes up, "Sharks are coming, so little fishes should run and hide!" The crier is a masked man wearing a **mullet** headpiece. "Beware, Shark is coming!"

Above: A "mullet" runs through the village with his attendants.

Below: Crowds of excited villagers gather on the riverbank to watch a very strange sight!

Above: The fisherman and his wife pursue Ofurumo, dragging their canoe on dry land.

Ofurumo

To the delight of all the spectators, floating down the river on a raft is *Ofurumo* [aw-FUR-uh-maw], or Shark. He is in a "cage," surrounded by musicians, drummers, and dancers. Close behind them, a fisherman and his wife paddle their canoe energetically in a **mock** fishing expedition. The crowd roars with laughter as the fisherman throws his spear at Ofurumo and misses—and the canoe **capsizes**!

Woe to the villagers, for Ofurumo reaches the shore and breaks out of his cage! But the fisherman and his wife continue their hunt on land. There is much rejoicing when they finally "spear" the wicked Shark.

Right: Ofurumo in his cage of wood and dry grasses.

13

Criminals beware!

The Ijo believe in powerful water spirits, and they represent these spirits in masquerades, with water spirit masks. A priest **invokes** these spirits on behalf of the villagers. *Eleke* [ay-LAY-kay] is one such spirit asked to settle disputes. Once the priest has called on Eleke to punish a criminal, the Ijo believe Eleke will begin killing the members of the guilty person's family. The only way to prevent more death is for the family to **sponsor** a masquerade to **appease** the water spirit.

Above: Eleke, his son, and his slave all mingle with the villagers. Here, Eleke's slave is playing with the people. The masquerade lasts for three days.

Right: The participants in the Eleke masquerade are, from left to right: the priest, Eleke's son, Eleke, and his slave.

Where land and water meet

The Ijo have lived along the waterways of the Niger Delta for hundreds, maybe even thousands, of years. Their festivals and masquerades show their close relationship with nature. In the past, while the river brought them food and water, floods and rains also caused much damage to crops and villages. Therefore, the Ijo regarded water as a powerful force. Some of these traditional beliefs survive today.

Many Ijo masquerades tell simple stories about the battle between good and evil. These celebrations often involve canoes and fish or beasts of the sea. Performances are **enacted** on the rivers, as well as on land.

Sharks are not the only animals featured on Ijo headpieces. This headpiece takes the form of a tiger fish.

Think about this

The Ijo depend on the river for many of their needs. Can you think of other cultures or peoples who also worship the forces of nature, such as the sun, wind, or rain? Who are some of these gods or goddesses?

FESTIVAL OF THE NEW YAM

Left: Do you like this dancer's colorful mask and costume?

Above: During festivals, the Igbo often draw beautiful patterns on their faces.

Many Nigerians are farmers, and harvest time is especially important to them. To ensure a good harvest, villagers organize festivals to honor the gods who look after the crops. The Igbo celebrate the Festival of the New Yam every year, just before the harvest begins. The festival honors the Earth goddess. If she isn't properly honored, she may refuse to help with the next year's crop, bringing famine to her people.

Preparing for the new year

The New Yam Festival is a time for getting rid of the old and starting over. Before the festival begins, the women clean their huts and decorate the walls with colored patterns. They scrub all the cooking pots until they shine. On the night before the festival, they cook all the yams left over from last year's crop. The new year must start fresh with only new, tasty yams. The women cook more than enough for all the guests at the next day's feast.

Above: A villager places the biggest and best yams before the chief, the man on the extreme right.

Right: An Igbo masquerade to ask for good crops. Which costume do you like best?

17

Eat, drink, and be merry!

On the first day of the festival, each family offers yams from the new crop to the Earth goddess and the ancestors, asking them for protection in the coming year. Friends and relatives visit from neighboring villages. Everyone spends the day feasting.

The women mark this special occasion by doing their hair and drawing **ornate** designs on their stomachs and backs. They also shave the heads of the children in beautiful patterns. Everyone dances the night away in masks or elaborate headdresses.

Right: Have you ever seen such a gigantic headdress?

Below: Children put on their masks and join in the fun during the New Yam Festival.

18

Time to wrestle

The second day of the festival is for wrestling matches. From early afternoon, the sound of drums can be heard all over the village. The drums remind the villagers of the excitement that awaits them. Toward evening, everyone gathers to watch the wrestling matches. Two teams of boys and young men line up across from each other. A wrestler from the first team dances across and picks the opponent he wishes to wrestle. They dance back to the center and begin the match. The last to fight are the two team leaders, the best fighters in the village. The winner will be carried off on the shoulders of the village men. For the rest of his life, villagers will remember his victory.

Think about this
Igbo men grow yams, while women grow all the other crops. An Igbo man's importance in the village is based on the size of the crops he grows. The yam harvest is a time that can make or break a man's reputation!

Cheer loudly for these brave boys! Hurray for the winner!

ID AL-FITR

Everyone is dressed up in their most colorful robes. They carry bright flags and umbrellas to shield themselves from the hot tropical sun. All around are bright colors, and everyone is in a festive mood. The procession leaves the city prayer ground and makes its way to the square in front of the **emir**'s palace. The emir and his troops bring up the rear. The emir takes his place on the throne. Horsemen from each of the surrounding villages take turns to charge toward the emir at full speed. They stop within inches of his throne and salute him with raised right fists. Last, and most impressive, are the emir's own bodyguards.

This man and his horse are on their way to salute the emir.

A sallah for Id al-Fitr

Above: Join this colorful procession to the emir's palace!

This form of charging salute is called a *sallah* [SAH-lah], a traditional way of honoring an important person. Nigerians might have a sallah anytime, but the best time is at *Id al-Fitr* [EED-ahl-FIH-tra]. Id al-Fitr celebrates the end of the 30-day fast of Ramadan. Muslims all over the world observe Ramadan. From dawn until dusk, for the entire month, they avoid eating or drinking. It can be quite difficult to go all day without water, especially when Ramadan falls during the summer months!

Right: A stunning display of horsemen charging across the square.

Left: Muslims kneel and bow in prayer during Ramadan.

Below: A group of Hausa women at the Id al-Fitr festivities.

Breaking the fast

During Ramadan, people wake up early to eat before sunrise. As soon as darkness falls again, they start a big evening feast. They also pay extra attention to prayers and to studying the Qu'ran (the Islamic holy book) during this time. When the new moon appears in the sky, it means Ramadan is over. It is time to celebrate the end of a successful fast. Everyone puts on their new clothes and goes to the mosque to pray. After the sallah, it is time for fun and feasting.

Nigerian Muslims celebrate Id al-Fitr with all kinds of fun activities. Here, people are watching a man taming a long-horned ox. This is a special version of a bullfight.

Who are these people?

Most of the people living in the northern part of Nigeria are Muslim. This part of the country is on the edge of the Sahara Desert. Long ago, camel **caravans** traveled across the Sahara to trade goods. Arab traders brought with them their religion—Islam. The Fulani converted to Islam. Then, they decided to bring their new faith to their neighbors and started a holy war. They conquered the Hausa and built an Islamic kingdom in what is now northern Nigeria. Today, the Fulani live with the Hausa. The two peoples share a faith in Islam and a love for horses.

Don't these Hausa girls look pretty in traditional dress?

Think about this

The sallah is not part of Islamic practices anywhere outside West Africa. It is one example of the many ways Nigerian Muslims have held on to traditional local customs and now use them in their religion.

THE ARGUNGU FISHING FESTIVAL

Every year, at the end of the growing season, the town of Argungu gets ready to celebrate. For days, the people have canoe races and swimming competitions. Drummers and dancers show off their skills. The high point of the festival, however, is the fishing competition. Fishermen come from all over the area to compete, and people come from all over the world to watch the action. For the rest of the year, this part of the Sokoto River is blocked off. No fishing is allowed, so there will be a great number of fish ready to be caught during the festival. Everything is set for the test that will show the best fisherman of all.

Rum-pum-pum! A man from Argungu drums up some excitement at the festival.

24

Above: Who will catch the biggest and heaviest fish of all?

On your mark!

First, there are opening prayers. Then, at the sound of a gun, thousands of fishermen dive into the swampy Sokoto River. Each holds a butterfly net in one hand and a calabash in the other. A calabash is a dried gourd Nigerians use like a jug. Soon, the water is crowded with fishermen, nets, and colorful calabashes. On the shore, drummers and singers create rhythm and music, adding to the festive atmosphere. The winner is the person who catches the largest fish. Competitors can use their nets, their calabashes, or even their bare hands to catch the fish. At the end of the day, a panel of judges weighs the fish and announces the winner. In 1997, the winning fish weighed a hefty 73 pounds (33 kilograms)!

Right: Could you catch a huge fish like this?

THINGS FOR YOU TO DO

The Edo live near the Yoruba in southwestern Nigeria. They have a special way of giving thanks for the good things that happen to them—they thank their heads! The Edo believe that "good heads" bring good fortune. To make sure things continue to go well, people bless their heads every year. They thank their heads for bringing them prosperity or good fortune. Then, they make any special requests they might have.

Using their heads and hands

The ancient Edo Kingdom of Benin was one of the most important kingdoms in Africa before the Europeans came. The people made many wonderful works of art that are still admired today. Some of the most beautiful ones show heads of rulers and other important people. Today, sculptors in Benin City in Nigeria make statues and heads in bronze and wood.

Make a head or a "hand of wealth"

Why don't you try using clay to make a model of your own head? The Edo used their bronze works to show the person's character. Try to make your clay model reflect your own strengths and qualities. The Edo also believe in the importance of a person's hand. The hand gives a person the strength to succeed in life. Chiefs sometimes carry on them a large hand made of cloth. This is called a "hand of wealth." Make yourself a hand of wealth and use it to give yourself a pat on the head!

Things to look for in your library

The African Mask. Janet E. Rupert (Clarion Books, 1994).
The Distant Talking Drum: Poems from Nigeria. Isaac Olaleye (Boyd Mills Press, 1995).
The Flying Tortoise: an Igbo Tale. Tololwa M. Mollel (Clarion Books, 1994).
Konkombe: Nigerian Music (video).
Nigeria (*Enchantment of the World* series). Dorothy B. Sutherland (Children's Press, 1995).
Nigeria: One Nation, Many Cultures (*Exploring Cultures of the World* series). Hassan Adeeb and Bonnetta Adeeb (Marshall Cavendish, 1996).
Yoruba Ritual (video). Margaret Thompson Dreval (Indiana University Press, 1992).

MAKE A DRUM

No Nigerian festival is complete without drums! Nigerian drummers create strong rhythms that add to the happy mood of their celebrations. Follow the simple steps on page 29, and you'll soon be ready for any Nigerian party!

You will need:
1. Two flowerpots
2. A piece of chamois
3. A thick cord 6 feet (1.8 m) long
4. Pieces of wire
5. A hole puncher
6. Scissors
7. Paintbrushes
8. A wax pencil
9. A bowl of water
10. A paint tray
11. Tempera paints
12. Four Popsicle sticks

1 Place the flowerpots base to base so the holes line up. Thread a piece of wire through one pair of holes. Wind each end of the wire piece around a Popsicle stick. Continue winding the wire until the sticks rest firmly at the bottom of each flowerpot. Do the same for all the sets of holes, until the flowerpots are held tightly together.

2 Paint bright designs on the flowerpots.

3 Cut the chamois in two circles, each 2 inches (5 cm) larger in diameter than the top of the flowerpot. Punch eight holes at regular intervals around the edge of the circles.

4 Wet the chamois. Put a piece over the top of each flowerpot. Knot one end of the cord, and thread the other through the holes, lacing the two pieces of chamois tightly together. Your drum is ready!

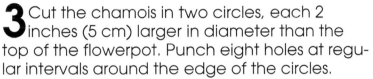

MAKE GINGER BEER

O n a hot day or during festive occasions, Nigerians like to cool down by drinking ginger beer. The drink is popular at parties and feasts, too. Treat your friends to a delicious, thirst-quenching glass of ginger beer!

You will need:

1. 1¹/₂ lb (670 g) fresh chopped ginger
2. 6 cups (1¹/₂ l) water
3. 2 cups (400 g) sugar
4. Seltzer water
5. Lemon slices
6. Ice cubes
7. Measuring spoons
8. A measuring cup
9. A glass
10. A large mixing bowl
11. A strainer
12. A metal spoon
13. A wooden spoon
14. A saucepan

1 Stir the ginger with the water and sugar in a saucepan. Simmer for 30 minutes, stirring occasionally. Let the mixture cool.

2 Strain the mixture.

3 Pour ¼ cup (60 ml) of the mixture into a glass. Fill the glass with seltzer water, a slice of lemon, and ice. Stir. This recipe makes 16 refreshing glasses of ginger beer!

GLOSSARY

appease, 14 — To satisfy, especially by giving in to demands.

capsizes, 13 — Overturns.

caravans, 23 — Groups of people or animals traveling together for safety, especially through the desert.

clan, 8 — A group of people, usually descended from the same ancestor.

destructive, 9 — Likely to cause or causing damage.

elaborate, 6 — Complicated; made in great detail.

emir, 20 — A ruler, prince, or commander in certain Muslim countries.

enacted, 15 — Acted out; performed.

invokes, 14 — Calls on, usually by chanting or special ceremonies.

masquerades, 6 — Festive gatherings of people wearing masks and costumes.

mock, 13 — Not real; pretended.

mullet, 12 — A small, edible species of fish.

ornate, 18 — Complicated in style.

sponsor, 14 — To pay for.

INDEX